Belt Loops & Bird Food
Collected Poems 2002-2009

Belt Loops & Bird Food
Collected Poems 2002-2009

By Elias Miller

pretend genius [press]
London, New York, San Francisco, Seattle, Washington D.C.

www.pretendgenius.com

Published simultaneously in the United States and Great Britain in 2009
by Pretend Genius Press
London, New York, San Francisco, Seattle, Washington D.C.

Copyright © Elias Miller 2009

This book is copyright under the Berne Convention
No reproduction without permission
All rights reserved.

ISBN 978-0-9747261-2-0

*To Debby, Sophie, Brooke, Marie, Kelly, Barbara, my mother
and the women who brought me to this point,
as well as the men who left me
to find my own way here.*

Contents

Preface	1
Bird Food	3
belt loops	4
single file	5
the villanelle from hell	6
poems chafe my butt	7
triangular	9
the last run	11
dear pru	12
2:28am Taipei Airport	13
the late breakfast	14
iraq track your way back	15
America... Uhhh... merica	16
no, where man?	17
your shoes	18
Let it snow	19
Epiphany	20
land of the free	21
death brings different socks	23
God the Stepfather	24
mother me	27
mantra	28
Remains	29
she sits	30
escape aid	31
Homecoming	33
Server Room	34
A Poem With No Adjectives	35
The Swimmer	36
the eye in sky	37
The Pain in Rain Falls Mainly on the Train	38
Progeny	39
Pen Ants, Pennants and Penance	40
Chapter Seven	41

settling in (a specular)	43
Intermission	44
Commute, No Commutation	45
A Poem Whose Title is a Little Longer Than the Actual Poem Itself	46
incubation	47
getting down in prairie dog town	48
new year new	49
dryheaving dastard's liniments (straddling poohs of derivity)	50
the end of the spectacle	52
ritualized	54
filler	55
the last gesture	56
Today I Threw You Away	57
The Wake Up	58
This Child of Nine-Eleven	60
Out Here	62
Hobo Sam	63
headline hangover	64
morning arrival	65
rapture redux	66
the pileup	69
this birthday	70
Nebraska (The Fall Back)	71
Awake in Dallas in the Light Hotel	72
not here (upstairs)	73
wandering beats	74
Night is a Casual Friend	75
the drift	76
exit	78
trance siberian	80
this thaw	81
there is music in hell	82

there sex is	83
stone mountain	84
Rubber Soles	85
Post Mortem	86
the shoreline	88
Spells	89
the crane pose	90
your new proportion will keep her happy	91
the face on the stairs	92
the common communion	93
holy rolled	94
Hightower's last meal	95
demotibilized	96
An American Stain	97
time warp	98
hungry	99
I have a nothing box	100
drive by	101
the end of poetry	102

Acknowledgement

"death brings different socks" and "God the Stepfather" appear in the poetry anthology "Last Night's Dream Corrected" from PretendGeniusPress. (ISBN: 978-0974726168)

Preface

I've always skipped reading any introductions in books, which makes it ironic that I would even want to write one for this publication. To me the introduction has never really been part of the text, only the filler at the front to annoyingly skip through to get to the "good bits". However, now that I'm on the other end of the book as the writer, I can see that this is where context and perspective can be set to enjoy the good bits. I hope you see it that way, but who knows. You may have skipped over this part already.

This collection has been made over the years, hopefully skimming the best of a body of work that has tracked my slow evolution as a writer. I have gravitated towards poetry partially due to my short attention span as well as the ability to compress meaning, create word play, soundscapes and generate impressions and insight in a small space. It has also been an outlet for those daily emotions that build over time until a poem can be created to release the pressure that arises. I suppose it is no different from anyone else's poetry in that respect.

In more recent times, these poems have become more concrete (and some have said better) as I learned to establish a context of common experience to anchor meaning and build an identification with the reader. For this skill, I have to thank all the various people through the MSN online writing groups that I have been participating in for the last 8 or so years. Their brutality, honesty and flippancy have helped me to let go of some of the preciousness I felt as an author to the words I risked putting out in the wilds of cyberspace. I also want to thank James, a published author, for effectively trashing my work a few years ago. Although I didn't write for a long time afterwards, what eventually came out was of a higher quality. I want to especially thank my wife and other key individuals who gave me feedback and directed me in this path of expression, currently the only indication that I'm actually a writer and not only a wannabe.

In any case, the experience and interpretation of these poem shaped words will be yours rather than mine. I may have written them, but you are the ones making the connections and seeing them form into visions and sensations. Poetry, once only the domain of the upper class and educated caste, is now a way for everyday people to see the world, to interpret the mundane into something deeper, perhaps even a universal identification of the human experience. Short of that, I hope these can provide at least some moments of entertainment and thought as your day pushes on as mundane as it can be.

Elias Miller
February 2009

Bird Food

Poems are pushy things
Never perfect, sometimes obtuse
Requiring dictionaries
Clarifications
Loose interpretations like a sack
Caught at the end of the morning's line
Only to be detached, examined
And thrown right back

The poem is a worm
Eaten by early birds
Words placed in sequence but out of sync
In ways that make dull heads think
Or ache
Language is broken to be remade
The poem is a bastard creation

Ever since we boxed up meaning
We made experiments to shake it
Crack it
Break it into halves
Wear it like hats when we're drunk and slurring
The blur of words churning in the bowl
Maybe it would be easier to unpack our feelings
And let them roll on the kitchen floor
Underfoot while we're cooking
And when no one's looking
We kick them squealing out the door

Poetry is for the birds
Let them pick over it on the lawn
And then before a sentence finishes
With flap of wings like applause
It's gone.

6/12/05

belt loops

bellhops topped with box hats stop,
cop a feel of cases, trunks,
dropped at the curb like an order
a border between legs straight and stumbled
jumbled over the din disgorged from metal buses

foreign faces float dull with fear
feel the carbon dust, the gust of smoke,
the choke of helpless dismemberment
as their cases of contained definitions
caravan conspicuously to the lobby
labial with comfort
red carpet lapping soles
sold to the unceasing tremolo of revolving doors.

3/24/02

<u>single file</u>

you've waited for this drum to snare
to stumble in its solo
and slip back to where you are.
the sun stares halfway tugged by the fisher's line
drawn up in time
to be served half-baked as humble pie,
don't know why you try to care

long walks thread through broom and gorse
among coarse paths under passive clouds
strung along by the claws of wind
that scrape into the shallow bay

i've seen the jagged way both coasts meet
beneath the quiet feet of the cross
while the master washes grime from his lands
and the dross of dusk dresses the hills
in its shroud of blank musk
masking the face of my borrowed time

my solo keeps it's steady pace
though slow to rhyme and seeming to pause,
your silence serves as accompaniment
though neither of us will mention the cause.

7/7/02

the villanelle from hell

see, even i can write a villanelle
every verse is plump with insight
life as a poet can be so swell

words can reek with a pungent smell
you can't discount a cliché's might
see, even i can write a villanelle

poetic form was a deep well
that's been plumbed until now each sortie's trite
life as a poet can be so swell

i'm so bewitched by this poem's spell
even reason's remnant has taken flight
see, even i can write a villanelle

is this poetry? time will tell
but boredom beds with my pen tonight
life as a poet can be so swell

until dawn i'll walk echelons of hell
reading this poem until sick with spite
see, even i can write a villanelle
life as a poet can be so swell.

7/28/02

poems chafe my butt

distraction
abstraction
contraction
reaction:

blah

i've dotted 'i' and crossed 't's
please please drag this on and on

i've not read anything for months on end
(end on months)

i need a good belch

i shop

pop

make me feel clever and smart
start a sentence with a verb
and end on a noun
sound like clown?

la la la

do bowlers bellow or do they blow below

yo ho ho

blocks are fun
they make walls
like the private ones in bathrooms stalls
or the cinder ones in dining halls
bench seating and a pot full of mash
smashed on a plate like an insult.
bollocks or flan?

i snore

george wallace's face practices smirks

i hate alliteration and assonance, mr. vance
but golfing makes me want to dance
in comfy golfing pants
clutching a 9 iron on the 11th hole

i'm not droll, but rather dry

sly dogs creep with slimy paws
why? because i want them to

i snore some more

what a bore
you chore
you good for nothing waste of space
placed poetically in front of thee

wheee!

(who says this is the final frontier?)
don't you dare come near, i'm almost done

there.

9/9/02

<u>triangular</u>

part three
three is a number
that most would say is odd
but rather it's uneven

she is sculpted
and behaves well when filmed.
her moles are for decoration
rather than for knowing.
she rocks her hips when she dances,
and i watch how her dress ripples
flashing smooth shins,
her eyes open halfway like a trance

part two
love works best in twos
but with three there's more to do

'beauty is a selfish thought.
it feeds upon itself, making its own hunger, until...'
behind the smoke of a gauloise
she pauses to check a nail,
'until you are a predator.'
the air swirls with a sigh.
'i am not your prey.
you want something i can never give.'
(i know where she will place the blow.)
'don't live with your empty plate extended.
feed me and i will feed you.'

part one
more ideological than practical,
one is the only thing that when multiplied by itself
equals itself.

thieves have been in my flat
and taken something warm away.
an impotent heater buzzes orange concern,

and i huddle beneath the wraps of covers
in cathode hues
remote in hand
repeating like a mantra
the deliberate motion of denial.

22/9/02

<u>the last run</u>

in a burst of expletives
you drove northward
and incognito crossed
the boundary of innocence
the border guards always smirking
as you chewed peppermint gum

the gun was in your purse
next to the pack of menthol newports
that paused unopened
waiting for you to run

and the door sounded heavy against your fist
(i too should have run)
you missed the first time
pulling rather than squeezing
but you aimed better when i pleaded.
you needed a reminder
as i did

half a pack down
you drive fast
leaving memory in your wake
the town lights sparkling in your rear-view
to the sound of rolling tires.

9/26/02

<u>dear pru</u>

do we care
do we care
that you wear your hair parted
or if you farted, daring to eat a peach?
(the newsreaders mumble each to each)

do we care do we care
if you sat there like a lump
sipping tea
staring at an arm
laying out spoons all afternoon
idolizing some fair tart like she was a blessing?
(her embroidered shawl is only window dressing)

think man think!
the yellow fog has blurred your sight
and given your matters importance beyond reason
(to each anxiety there is a season)
so how should you presume?
marriage can be no better than being alone
and some might say worse
so don't curse and drone on like you were in hell
you live well, your mind is not slow
(thought not as talented as michelangelo)
so how should you presume?
think of those who long to eat,
who dreams comprise of cakes and ices
(can you really force this moment into a crisis?)

in truth to the world you matter not
nor do i
so let's have a pint at a sawdust bar
and maybe a cry for our lost pride
from when we thought we had importance
to merit an epic poem or two
(perhaps a eulogy will have to do.)

9/29/02

2:28am Taipei Airport

The wireless LAN hub flickers
Next to the block figure toilet sign
Black vinyl chairs rest in rows back to back
Unburdened from asses and baggage

The cleaning lady wears a yellow vest
Her life jacket from the ocean of faces that could be here
Filling the hall
With coughs
Spit
Scuffs
She erases the thought with her mop
Flicked in almost Soviet automation

Sparse foreigners faze to headphones
But she focuses on the floor
Where countless soles have passed
And left their dark residue.

11/20/02

the late breakfast

the glottal pot boils its eggs
licked by the stove flame
hissed from iron pores
like stores of estrus discharged
drawn by the promise of fire,
the pyre of passion that cooks time

you observe with scientific thought
caught in the eddies of untruth implied
by your mother's false advice
as she lied to get you outside the kitchen on saturdays
to swing under the grays of the autumn sky

and today is one such saturday
though once your eggs are stirred and cooked
and the flame shut
you stand in your robe facing away
eyes cut by the mid-morning light
waiting for the steam to disperse like a falsity.

3/17/03

<u>iraq track your way back</u>

5
'ultimatum' is a tyrant's word
poised on the itch of a trigger finger
on the boy who would be man
who tacks a smirk to his furrowed brow
while the camera slow tracks forward in awe
no word of what his father saw,
only slogans to justify his cowboy propensity
like a jacksonian bully in a sandbox
defining democratic 'manifest destiny'

4
goddam saddam rhymes in (and with) alabama

3
rumsfeld's bum smelt of fenugreek
as he yielded diplomacy's citrus aurantium
and then forgot his handshake
only to return in six years to claim it back

2
there is oil to be had and industry to be won
there are inroads and back roads
commercial footholds in hostile places
iraq backs onto a swarthy doorstep
don't the towel-heads need goods too?
so what's the fuss over UN resolutions
that pass like moot conclusions shrugging benign concern
let's earn, let's control,
(let's patrol the back alleys with soldiered guns)
and then the fun really starts

1
4pm Thursday, Pacific Standard Time,
"Showdown Iraq", brought to you by Ocean Fresh Tide,
turning the tide against the war on dirt.
and now here's our correspondent Wolf Blitzer...

3/19/03

America... Uhhh... merica

Night and day the bombs punctuate
Exclamations of hot expletives
Pock mark walls
Potholes the size of buses
Building trusses shudder blazed with blast marks
Dark streaks like morbid blush
Traffic jams of Bradleys and Abrams blazing dust

Rubble crushed bodies laze beside saline drips
Maimed children missing legs
Mothers ululating grief
Brief glimpses of calm under fossil fuel smoke
Soldiers toke the pungent air wearing camouflaged stone
Reporters hone their skills for the ratings war
Civilian casualties soar into the thousands

We say we came to liberate,
But when they see our rockets red glare
And bombs bursting in air
They will pray for us take the oil and leave.

4/4/03

<u>no, where man?</u>

after midnight, the heater glow is all I know
its dark orange, like amber monochrome
makes sepia of my room
an empty desk backs against the wall
bordered by black
a snapshot of classic solitude.

6/12/03

<u>your shoes</u>

these eyes have seen your shoes crusted with siberian mud scuffed on the sidewalk during a temperature snap. they've seen dog's breath hang in the air waiting for the clap of a passerby to shoo it away. they've seen brick walls showing cracks, dark tags, the bags of potatoes with eyes that see nothing. histories pass over eyes, over the stare of black snow. no one knows where it will go. who is the hero? who will make amends? who will falter and eat chocolate cake and freeze in the street. who will you meet? who will you forget? these eyes have ridden beside you in third class on a russian train, burning with smoke and smells of entrails on bread. fish eggs and pickled onions sat in jars on the sill. traders filled their bags with chinese wares, plastic dolls, counterfeit walkmans, cheap jeans - anything they could sell. a drunkard took out a swedish porn mag from his coat. a child clutched her naked barbie doll to her chest. two pale youths smoked bulgarian fags by the sliding door. you wrote "pillock" on my arm with your ballpoint when i spilled my tea. this is all history. this place doesn't exist anymore. you don't exist anymore. only your shoes you once wore are left here to remind me.

5/19/04

<u>Let it snow</u>

It has snowed for three days
And trees bow down in humility
Monochromatic scenes outside chilled windows
Remind me of ski trips spent in the car
Chains beating the roads
Behind a string of taillights
Rows of red eyes staring

The world is colder today
Coated with this shroud
Clouds blend with the ground
And the sound of life is muffled
Like a vow of silence
Stuffed into our gaping mouths.

8/17/04

Epiphany

From the moment I saw you
In the condiment aisle
Hand on the mustard
I knew
You were the one
To invite
To my barbeque.

8/27/04

land of the free

freedom is a mirage
freedom is a poor man's catch-phrase
freedom is a lever for the ignorant
freedom is a carrot on a string
freedom is a whip on broken skin

america is no more free than the soviet union was
america doesn't want freedom
america wants ordered voracious consumers,
independently wealthy money-makers,
happy service industry slaves
and wide-eyed watchers of tv.
"a well balanced breakfast is toast, juice, milk and cereal."
have you ever mixed juice and milk?
can you say lobbies, kickback, and campaign contributions?

people are upset by this thought
they act surprised and outraged as if their sacred cow was shot
they've marched for freedom
fired guns for freedom
formed hate groups for freedom
stuffed their faces for freedom
made porn for freedom
killed foreigners for freedom
given up civil liberties for freedom
and the media watched it all and recorded every second
"god bless america," they yelled,
"land of the free (spending)
and home of the brave (sports enthusiast)"

americans don't really want freedom
they want comfort
and there's comfort to be had
at a price
and that price is their freedom
and the freedom of the rest of the world

freedom is the smell of one new empty shoe
freedom is the promise of desert rain

freedom is a willing chain of slavery for the poor
freedom is a fireworks display
freedom is a scapegoat
freedom is a christmas tree
freedom is a slot machine jackpot

freedom is just a lullaby.

9/13/04

<u>death brings different socks</u>

bilirubin makes up for your lack of asian genes
as the sunlight writes your name in shadows
now made more even as breathing slows
or as thinking slows.
who knows?

closets full of unworn clothes
compete for space as we cram ourselves
between drawers of tube socks and the leaky loo
twelve years a bachelor marked out in chili cans and condensed soup
finally you've flown the coup
and women flock to clean up after you

your youngest son builds the box
(which we wipe down with your socks)
and your oldest waits for you to look with recognition
but by your own admission
you lived for years waiting to be seen
as you hid on Sand road behind the cedar hedge
the radio always on in case the world ended without you

they say that death comes with a rattle
but it sounded more like socks stuffed in a box
and the muffled sense of loss
when you give away something you never really had

though we plan to bury you
to the sound of taps under a triangular flag
we bury the memories of all we missed
the dad that came and left but liked to hover
like an aloof eagle in the sky
occasionally swooping before he said goodbye.

9/28/04

"I have two fathers,
Two Gods
One dead and the other dying
Part of one whole
The Stepfather, the son, and the only ghost."

<u>God the Stepfather</u>

He came into my life unbidden
Moving carefully so as not to disturb my toys
And like Zeus seduced my mother while I slept

He spent time talking to me about school,
About logic and perspective
And I could see how His beard covered pockmarks.
His youth let Him down,
And He needed to hide it

The times He pressed His lips until white
(and the strike seemed not far behind)
I hid in His broken Thunderbird
Parked in the garage next to the stacks of old Playboys

His own son visited,
Sometimes a Tom and others a Thomas,
He was the first to show me a centerfold
Wearing nothing but a pink sunhat and red platform shoes
Pink nipples and orange pubes.
I didn't understand why he left his door ajar
And spent Saturday mornings under his covers.
He wanted us to play make believe
Where he was the queen and I was the subject.
He asked me for worship from my mouth
And I couldn't.
I wasn't his servant

My mother wanted more than me
Because my father gave her four (and she lost three)
But she wouldn't take what Stepfather had
At age nine, I visited her in the ward.
Her barren womb removed,

He couldn't make her whole

He used to give me commands
And taught me right from wrong
But mostly I saw He lived above His Law.
He trained me to hate what He hated
And hate what He loved
And I learned
I ate like He did
I ate to escape
And I rebelled
Quietly

I followed His doctrine
Dictated by guts and genitals
Sentimental and penitent
Pleasing the strongest impulses to surface
Always unable to numb desire.
Like an oil fire
My smoke filled the sky

He is older, powers fading,
Faster now that my dad is gone
Ineffable and ineffectual
Slowing and swerving
Clinging to the steering wheel

And I see my end in His end
I see my eyes in His
The dusty books in wooden shelves
Discarded tools filling the workshop
Boxes of memories among the rats
Eaten slowly, growing holes,
His reason stolen by the gnaw of hours

The house He built needs care
Mother waits for Him
She knows where He is
And He knows why
But will He pass below her
Under the bricks and concrete His hands have touched
Into the rest that waits like hole

Sucking at Him until He's small enough to swallow
Leaving His ghost to keep her thoughts warm

I'd ask Him for forgiveness
But He'd just make excuses,
His behavior beyond reproach,
Outline burned like a shadow,
Face glowing in the cathode light
Clicking away the moments that remain.

9/20/04

mother me

stand straight
speak clearly
wait to be spoken to
talk to me
listen
be nice
be honest
never say my age
how old is she?
don't stare (but look at her over there)
don't ummm or ahhh
be good
be better than everyone else
don't act better than everyone else
be polite
shut up
speak up
be quiet
don't slouch
don't worry
don't be angry
be careful
take off your shoes
put on your coat
look out
stay in
stand still
hurry up
slow down
close your mouth
say something
don't interrupt
look at me
don't stare at me
speak to me
don't talk to me like that
don't lie

do you miss me?

10/20/04

<u>mantra</u>

i will live to see the day we return from the landfill clutching a gum wrapper and piece of string
i will live to see the day the serpent rises from my bed and devours me in two bites before watching 'jeopardy' reruns.
i will live to see the day you bring flowers and a blue plastic vase to the pta meeting
i will live to see the day my face withers and sags in the summer heat
i will live to see the day you look at me and think of derelict whitewashed fences
i will live to see the day my children point to me and say "it was his fault"
i will live to see the day i open my mouth and ink drips from my tongue onto your embroidered doilies
i will live to see the day my past is summed up in a single snapshot
i will live to see the day the stars fall to earth and all property values rise
i will live to see the day i forget my name and stand at the signpost at the bottom of the world and see nothing but the pacific ocean breaking over the volcanic stone and spraying mist over my technicolor windbreaker
i will live to see the day i open a box with my name on it and see it empty

all this all this all this all this
is nothing more
and nothing less.

10/20/04

Remains

The radio crackles though wood grain speakers
And I laze with the windows open
Sunlight drowsing flies until they walk
Pictures fade in a glare on the west wall

The cedar tree in the front yard tips towards the house
Roots sprawled in the heat clasp spongy earth
The low roof glances down in silence
To where tomato vines once clung to string

The small bedroom feels hollow
With the mattress lying on the floor
Empty closets behind closed doors resound
The last footsteps in this final act

Cracked weatherboards patched for the sale
Are pale with their mask of paint
Memories that remain faint sketches when covered
Read like stories in the dents and etches

Those with history here can see them
Even the ones burned in the rusted oil barrel
And the sound of almost feral bursts of laughter
Recalled by the ears and nerves who heard

For the man who lived here died here
And left his soul here
Mainly in the dried lawn cut while it was green
And in the screen of a hedge encircled like a fortress wall
That made the map of the known world
The brutal world
Feel more assuring and small.

12/13/04

she sits

she twists her hair until it binds her hand
in the scuffed corner of some espresso dive
not quite alive but still smoldering,
ember poised over a bland paperback
shades in place despite the hour

panhandlers grope the outer tables.
aware of their approach
she moves her purse with her feet
without changing her stare
her brown strands stay wound like a rope

i glance over my copy of "the stranger"
shifting my chair with unease
her pale knees closed as if asleep
the breeze from a fan
shuffles smoke from her face
the place where interest should be
is erased from memory

i circle the word 'deceased' to remind me
just as brown foam on the rim of my coffee bowl
the past is a hole that prowls like the haze of dead cigarettes
wiping yellow residue on walls and over eyes
before it lies at your feet and growls when you move.
she watches it linger with the last of her storyline

a late bus groans by with a howl of air
and the waiter starts his wipe down
the town barely slows in the dark.
the glow of coffee hues the skyline
as mercury halos spotlight sooty figures
passing absently beyond the glass

i find no excuse to remain
but she feigns a dream state
insect eyes affixed on the horizon,
a model's pose awaiting immortality.

1/13/05

<u>escape aid</u>

we count our moments in rotations
each lifting of the phone
each dial tone
these hone our purpose to a keen glint:
cutting the strands of rope
to defeat her noose
loose our hands
and give us hope for rotations to come

we walked to the estuary down ferry road
over gravel shoulders by the sea wall
seaweed sprawled on bare rocks
seagulls dotted the mud of low tide.
you almost cried at the thought of leaving
(i would have seen the pain in your eyes
but your shades were in place)
i've watched traces of your sorrow harden as they fall
blown by the train of cars that rushed by

the sun hid behind clouds as we pushed further on
to the triangular hub of mccormack's bay
we took the road away from cars
and stared at houses we would never own
some maintained and others overgrown
with grasses tall and matted through pickets
fences split and chipped and mostly bare.
we would never live there,
nor on the sheer face of mount pleasant

in a park our daughter toddled along a low stone wall
chewing on pine cones and bark
leaving her own mark on nature
never knowing the choices we face
ones we might have to erase or at least forget.
she has long to learn about regret.
she paced towards us and then away
this is her game
and we laughed along as we looked beyond to the chill water
and watched the sun stare at us sideways

in the afternoon's end we walked one loop, one turn,
your fair skin burned in the bright march day
but rather than stay cooped up in four walls
we pushed the pram and moved our feet
only to face again our last home
our transit lounge at the start of fall
before the final boarding call.

3/17/05

Homecoming

Days run between my fingers like sugar spilling on the floor
I don't think much anymore
Just move my limbs to the tick of my motor
Engine sputtering mid roar

I've thrown out years of decisions
Dumpsters full of broken plans and decay
Half eyeglasses, dead pens, rat torn bindings
All this detritus was left in my way

I'm here in this half land
Half dark and half felt
Lured by the promise of goods
Hoodwinked by the blink of the illumined eye
The clink of change in my lined pockets
Stocked with fine weaves and perfumes
Exhumed from the back mind
Always watching with his mouth open

The fingers of trees have been cut back
The grass mown, the weeds sprayed
I stayed too long away
Drawn by the promise of arms
Where seeds were sown
Gophers burrow unimpeded,
Their number unknown.

6/18/05

<u>Server Room</u>

Network cables dangle on the wall in a stranglehold
Florescent lights flutter their dull eyes
To roars of servers stacked side by side
And thighs of boxes pried apart and thrown in a pile,
All the while the night shuffles in keyboard strokes
Spoken in the corner while monitors doze
And tokes the ozone behind the red eye
Colon blinks of the coiled black phone.

8/16/05

A Poem With No Adjectives

My daughter wept when we left her room
And screamed protests through the walls
Her code of distress
Each rise and fall a plea
Fingers clinging to the crib
Calling daddymummy.

9/18/05

The Swimmer

There is a poem swimming naked
In the backwaters of my head
Her steady strokes belie strong verbs
With soft adjectival curves
And nerves of emotive filament

This poem skinny-dipped its way
Across my brain in stark plainness
Until noticed by my pen.
Then with dark currents
I drew her towards the shore
To be seen and heard by men.

9/18/05

the eye in sky

i check my watch and see it's time.
the stare of a blue iris ringed with white
hogs hours onscreen despite the brightness of these stars

the said divine curve of wrath cuts a path to the south
and chases away pillars of cars.
the math indicates a progression to destroy
like the spinning tantrum of a stifled boy
a circumference that knots of escapees attempt to avoid

devoid of meaning, clouds gather and disperse.
cookie crumbs fall into my shirt folds,
cursed with a slow thyroid
and annoyed by the drone of speculative voices,
i toy with my choices to weather the onslaught or flee
but when i return
will anything be left of me?

9/21/05

The Pain in Rain Falls Mainly on the Train

I'm a responsible citizen.

I walk to the train station and join the queues of proletarians who, like me, are objecting to the problem of inflated petrol prices precipitated by perpetual meddling in the political affairs of Middle Eastern peoples by pro-west politicians. We are proud of our pertinent civil-service minded gesture as we ourselves save money from the evil of corporate domination. We cycle. We recycle. Michael rows his boat ashore on our isle of righteousness. We spawn our own resistance against the system that confines us, tricks us, anesthetizes us and imprisons us. Do not be wavered by the offers of employee discounts on fuel-hungry SUVs. We save the planet. We wear hemp sandals and compost our green waste. We taste like granola and smell like a joint. We point the finger at corporatocracy and greed. Heed us. Join us. Weave baskets and discover macramé with us. Walk, bike and ride the bus. Vote with your bare feet. We suffer so that others can live. We won't conform because we are free. Be like us or beware. Don't buy or wear clothes from the Gap. We are for peace, but we won't take your crap. We're ready for the revolution. If need be we will take over by force. We are on course. Soon the world will be ours and our children will be named Rainbow and Plain.

We take the train, and our pain is mainly felt in the rain.

10/27/05

Progeny

My daughter is a simulacrum of me.
Enough dark hair and olive skin
For strangers to say to my wife
"Is her dad Italian?'
When she walks with her on the way to the store
Down Mt Diablo Boulevard.
My wife with green eyes and red hair
And fair skin and replies,
"How did you know?"
While my daughter waves at them until they smile.

11/5/05

Pen Ants, Pennants and Penance

Some days I don't want my friends or these ligaments that bind me
Religion finds me under the pew by the worn shoes of parishioners
Smelling of fish and stained with blood
Wishing Jesus saved the good chewing gum and crumbs
Crushed by the shuffle of soles
Wet with drips of holy water
Pressed through holes ripped in pant knees
By the shiny feet of daughters and sons
Who got dragged to the dogma house and didn't leave

I grieve for the lost days spent confined in the confessional
Chafing at my collar
Heavy hands on my shoulders
Waiting for the guilt to disrobe me.

11/18/05

<u>Chapter Seven</u>

I.
I spent nights over cups of coffee
Laughing at the way my skin inches down
Watching the late acts in wayward bars
The bare stragglers choking on smoke
Dull eyed, black eyed, christened by the dead
Dreams of endless head and breasts
In electric reproduction sucked by red globes
Bare lobes distressed with guitar distortion
The motion of living drawn from each drag
Fags with fags gagging on virtual cocks
Beneath Big Al's socks and the serpent,
Rome's steps only seconds away

II.
Chinese steam puffs through beaten doorways
Where sideways looks mingle with fried duck
And cheap goods fuck in garish display.
I stray far from the main road
Walking like a folding chair
John street, Bush street
Up Nob hill and down again.
Victorian buildings stacked like dominoes,
Casual hoes hang their wares,
Staring with pill eyes, strutting slow.
They catcall me and I know their bodies,
I know their souls,
Sagging and shrinking, sucked at by coffins
Promises of nothing, often,
Followed by leers of grief and sorrow
Their legs are borrowed and thrown aside,
The Seeing Eye stuffed into damp brassieres

III.
O'Farrell playbills decorate abandoned walls
By the beggars sleeping in cardboard stalls
The pall of filth living in their creases
The city survives in patches of grime
Smeared by time over pieces of sleeping bags used as coats
And coats used as shirts

And shirts as rags for their feet.
Bums hold out their hands and I look at them blind

IV.
The city greases its lips in the reflection of the black bay

V.
Shame puddles in dark pools on Market Street
As cars choke the artery with eyes glowing
Always flowing in a huddle against the unknown hurt outside
Strangers never meet and part ways forever.
Humans enjoy a good slide by themselves
Until they land in dirt

VI.
I take my ride and leave by the east bridge.
The ridge of hills is the refuge
I refuse to leave behind.
The Caldecott hole is orange and warm
And already I feel clean
With the murky bay behind me

VII.
I spent nights over cups of coffee
Laughing at the way my skin inches down
To the dark town, the dirty town
Where promises of nothing are often kept
Close to the yellow fog
That circles the city like a crown.

11/24/05

settling in (a specular)

i let your call go to voicemail
call-waiting is a boon to the timid
refusing to talk, not wanting to fail,
i spent the day putting away my things

cardboard boxes dissolve into trash
with rash choices like crumpled paper
half of which i left behind
from the days i wasted waiting for your smile

the garage shelves are stacked with old files

from the days i wasted waiting for your smile
half of which i left behind
with rash choices like crumpled paper
cardboard boxes dissolve into trash

i spent the day putting away my things
refusing to talk, not wanting to fail
call-waiting is a boon to the timid
i let your call go to voicemail.

11/27/05

Intermission

Dark circles underscore December eyes
Your naked thighs, a reverse envelope
I would kiss you, but my stubble will graze
Your nipples point out my strengths
Wait until I have yet spoken,
Then interrupt me in waves.

12/8/05

Commute, No Commutation

Morning cars line up for the green
Farting steam, sweating, dripping, bleary headlights staring
Each a muffled dissonance of radio vibrations
Each a branded appellation

I walk in the carbon-monoxide mist,
The frost still gripping broken grass
In yellow patches where dogs pissed.
The fogged glass of commuters
Pushes past the congested gas station
To pull into a glutted parking lot
Near the dull hum of the train tracks

I have no hat
So I shrug in my wool coat
And trace the slow curve of the street.
Cars shuffle and queue
Like cows soon to be meat.
People pre-packed in their Christmas boxes
Are conveyed by this concrete rut
Butt to nose to butt
To their transit destination

I mumble my thoughts by the frozen park.
The swings still and the tan bark
Clumps in mounds around dark earth.
Children grounded by the season
Are at home eating Cheerios near the heater vent
Bent over the bowl, cupping cold orange juice.
Sensible parents click the TV remote
And drink coffee in morning robes

My lobes become numb
As I make my way to the bus without parental fuss
On the strip of grey tongue that unrolls like a welcome
Into the gullet of December.

12/9/05

<u>A Poem Whose Title is a Little Longer Than the Actual Poem Itself</u>

A Panda sticks bamboo
Between its teeth
And mutters,
"Shoot me."

12/15/05

incubation

many things i want to write are not right
so they sit in the back mind
knitting wool scarves
plucking their brows
acting like cows or even cats
catching rats
burrowing through cracks
at the back of old bindings
chewed clean in the basement cold

loose threads are tied in a knot
when hot words boil meaning from the open pot
only when flesh starts to burn there is steam
and screams of words splutter red.
dead letters speak when dissected
the page is the only evidence of the crime

my time is paid out in hours
warming this chair
thinking of flowers opening in the light
in the right conditions defined by whim.
pins of morning air
prick the shape of a voodoo sign
outlined in dim reflections on the office wall.
divine conscience is dulled incrementally with disuse

two chairs are empty by the door
the whiteboard stares with few words to say
motion sensor lights click off though i sit here
pushing all the keys
pleading, please please
bring me to my knees
but not so hard as to make me crawl
i'd rather stand and kneel than fall
on these old slabs forced together
by the memories of cold hands.

12/19/05

getting down in prairie dog town

"One litter is born to the Prairie Dog female each year. During a 4 or 5 hour estrus, a female Prairie Dog may mate with as many as 5 different males, allowing pups from the same litter to have different fathers...."

three hundred and sixty four and three quarters days
men wander the streets
keeping watch, digging tunnels
training the young to burrow and bark
funneling tension in the occasional run
marking time in feedings and rest
and watching the sky like a widescreen tube.
the best shows distract libidos.
no fantasizing about fat rolls,
fur holes,
or willing bodies flopped languidly on the dirt;
only one channel with clouds and the fiery ball circled by hawks

desert sunsets don't inspire romance here.
stars never flirt with cynomis nocturnal hopes.
teenage couples don't park at the point,
and no admission to any emissions
when young males are alone in the dark

there are no bordellos, no bitches of the night
no bar fights over possible mates
or hooning in tricked out cars
or flashy threads, cheap scents
or posturing over size.
the men realize this means nothing.
jealousy and loss are not immortalized in song.
there are no long engagements or promises of love,
no child support or requirements to pay the rent
no dances or chances or even luck

for once the waiting time is done
all the females want to fuck.

12/20/05

new year new

explode fireballs after orbs dropped with shiny markers between numbers flipped on six channels with regis and half-brained dick slurring diabetic discoballs and tongues catching confetti to jutting hips and drunk cops patrolling cleavage gowns split in even halves sequined slits wet with banter swaggering talent greased for cameras sliding between legs of years spitting cigarettes into gutters churning trash party hats twirled from expectations with new orgasms thrust froglike in dark armpits stumbled over sidewalks of vomit puddles splattered in beer spray again again spray beer in splattered puddles of vomit sidewalks over stumbled armpits dark in froglike thrust orgasms new with expectations from twirled hats party trash churning gutters into cigarettes spitting years of legs between sliding cameras for greased talent swaggering banter with wet slits sequined halves even in split gowns cleavage patrolling cops drunk and hips jutting to confetti catching tongues and discoballs diabetic slurring dick half-brained and regis with channels six on flipped numbers between markers shiny with dropped orbs after fireballs explode.

1/1/06

dryheaving dastard's liniments (straddling poohs of derivity)

slumber sticks to me like oil
dark graffiti for my eyes
pulls my fingers into light sockets
tangential to tangerine tangiers tarrantino tangled
queers quell quills quick my underpants are burning
this sicks to ficks the licks a;laskf laksdjf laskjfa;slkfj
i am boring snoring whoring touring blustering
a dullard with map but no wish to burn brun brum
what do ia wanna do wap dee doo doo

she's short on love but long on sex talk
where's my chequebook
fix me some eggs and lox my beechwood birch
could you hand me down a beggar bowl
my penis (or should i say crotch) is buried in the dirt pillorying this confounded vine
in vitreous veneer involving venomous vitruvian vaginosis

alamanda connuculus tweaks her full cleavage until it resembles her ass
until she forgets if she's coming or going (but usually coming)
buttressed against the butler's butter churner with pneumatic accuracy
delicate digitalis substitutes kidney filters
her liver spots lurk under bleach paste
she preens in her pink party dress
coke snot dribbling the scar of her harelip
post nasal drip slipping after the xanax and cognac chaser
she flips her compact and checks the jagged rip of her lipstick luscious lolling perfect

dastard testiculi rocks the foxtail doorknocker mocking shave-n-a-haircut rhythms
jisms in his chinos a propos to his flimsy flick hairdo ego
ergo he knows he's devastatingly erect effecting felonious fellatio fanfares
alamanda knickerless flicks on the porch light shaped like a pendulous boob
lubes her crotch wrap with cool whip slapped on like a butter boat
coaxes the sticky deadbolt closed then open then closed again
a house shag is always better when desire distills into determined dust devils

dastard pulls open his blue van heusen button-down and yanks his nipple ring
sings volaré and swings his pendulous perfunctory hosebead
until passing out from oxygenation deficit
falling following doric delineations ironic into the holly bush

crushing his plush hush puppies with dismorphic rushdies

alamanda eyes her peep show and oils the hinges before opening the door hole
"damn ghost knockers" she mutters and unclasps her cross-your-heart bra
drool dribbles her double chin while she buffs her king clovis crown
corsair whips her wet harelip in the moonlight until it gleams

pristine chris green drives by pissed on listerine
observes the scene in the bordello whoreway
and careens into a doily store totaling his volvo squareback
virgo houses his yugo yogurt until he un-tangos from his wreck
peckering the path with the crumbs of nutterbutters
peanut paste smacking the lipscombe larder tongue stuck to his palatial pope dome
"lllluhhhh lmlmhhhll llllluhhh" he mutters lovingly to alamanda's nylon knickerbockers
"well?" alamanda spits in his eyes and spies his lugubrious lovelorn lollygagger
"lllllllllllllllllllllllllll!" he lists about wringing fists and pinching his nip-tucks
"twenty bucks!" she beckons with her latex fuscia beef pole towards the pink hole in the cupola.
he drags his tripod tiddlywinks towards telltale titillation through the doorway
disrobing in flirtatious strips ripped in rope lengths across the foyer.

alamanda connuculus and chris green vaginate vacillate vegetate until daybreak
fossilizing in the deep freeze when the axis flips
and end up as stone chips in the terramundo excavation display on argos 3 circa lun 23059030
admission by free donation of 45 dsplicaboijs to the overlone musalero preldibabthoerean
where the tour guide snores these immortal words:
askdhj aioh aweroiv aoiej alksnadonfwenlkdsfjod
asdflkasls sadflkj owiej dsifj oasd
asdfoijaweoij sfa
asnklsdf
adslk ho.

1/9/06

the end of the spectacle

blowflies flit their wings and ovulate
maggotizing flesh in the midst of august nuptials
the first blush of dead blood
on its journey to becoming dust
(nothing more than liquid rust, i'm told)
though the repetition is getting old

in paris they pray for a giant cunt
to fuck the eiffel tower once and for all
in st louis they pray for the arch to fall
in san francisco that god will crush the golden gate
and light will expose these late wonders
as nothing more than a publicity stunt

gog and his dog eat pecan pie at nations
his jaw filled with fish hook fights
washed with libations of soda water wine
hermaphrodite whispers fill skirt hems and straps
sidewalks crack under herr man's weight
promises of sex annexed by gomer's fear
queer pushes jumping sawhorses before gun shots
riddled with folded foreskin fumbled poses
dry humping, wet humping,
pumping pneumatic dna male delivery

love sumps lick the foam from stiff fomentation
next of kin postulate reprobate morticians
drain the hose blood, refill the skin
pack the dead to suit the living's nose
with vitriol octane for the revival

the savior swills his miller lite
and satan savors a coffeemate enema before the fight,
the faceless place their bets with cardinal bookies
confessions are at an all time high
so are thighs opened to receive penance
fragrances by mennen leap off the shelves
as obsession sales drop into the abyss
the great reversal as foretold
bold strokes of visionary fools

retooled by market forces felt in wall street

god is like a corporation dispensing libations to the creation
too broad for the market?
how about:
god - everything you've always wanted in a beard, and less...

1/9/06

ritualized

i placed my trust in her
my thrust in her
her bust bronzed and unforgiving
she only stares at my profile
preferring plato to plotinus

her divinity was just a phase
assigned by guilty assignations
motivations to repair
the heat she dissipated
into the dusty books she preferred over me

the bird of madness flaps wet wings
and sings in the cloudy mirror.
shower steam swirls like fog,
streams of blood left to memory
drained into pipes and smoked before dawn

marble ashtrays now empty
weigh down the polished wood
echoing to the two step
genuflection at her glossy altar

with her gone i preserved what i could
and now she is good for ritual.

2/10/06

<u>filler</u>

this is not a poem
a love song or even a verse
this is not a curse
or an epithet or vilification
this is not a depiction
or even a description
this is not fiction
or fact or anything completely true
this is just a pile of words
filling the space
where i used to see you.

5/30/06

the last gesture

"sex is redundant," you liked to say
after the kisses and foreplay were done,
the sway of old seduction rocking me in a wave

pressing your hand into your folds,
you climaxed as i stood to leave,
the steam blinding me like fog

i watched you lie on the duvet
a sculpture only meant for display
your dry hand half caressing your thigh

"thy wit is spent," you turned to say,
but the wick, without flame,
had smoked its last goodbye.

6/2/06

Today I Threw You Away

In the piles of papers and letters
The stacks of square notes you scrawled
The physics books, the math books,
The dated pamphlets in triplicate,
From the hard candies to the soft socks
I hauled you to the dumpster and threw you away

Today I coughed what was left of your dust
And sneezed it out into your cave
The white walls your pre-grave
Silent after countless clicks and stares.
Your folded chair cold
Despite the hours you played Freecell

Today I threw out your old life
Your first wife, your first son
Paid one of your parking tickets
Chucked your debris:
The stash of one-armed reading glasses
The 1945 Lubbock yearbook
The broken ukulele

I squeezed you out
I wrung you out
I washed and wrapped you
And put you in a box.
I threw you away.
I crushed what was left of you,
Crumpled what was left
Smashed and folded and shredded
Your post partum remains.
I destroyed what was left of your chains

And today
You are free to go.

7/31/06

The Wake Up

Got to get down these moments of clarity
These pieces of me on greasy cloth seats
The train riders half asleep
Despite electronic dings and jolts of electricity
Thirty years of diseases and dirt
Left by countless soles rubbing the rug under their feet
Thrive with each minute of human humidity

The sycophantic backs that circle
The sycophantic backs that stare
Swing their slow legs
Dressed in tidy threads
Business threads still absent of sweat
Shiny with iron marks
Dull in the daylight of the clouded windows

The gray sky turns and shies away
From the lengths of cars speeding towards the hills
The tunnel beckoning suggestively

I have ruminated about life
Over the click clack of tracks
Fluoresced until my eyes watered
Begging for sleep until my head waggled
Watching lines of people wander towards leftover empty spaces
The fat, the thinning, the old, the aging
Staging their way through measured spans of time
Transitioning through double-doors to the next car to find a seat
Forgetting their daily decay until they are reminded

This morning I watch their groggy thoughts stumble and slip
After toothbrush automation
As a prelude to sunglasses half-asleep shaken open by the ride
Their demands are just keys to be pushed repeatedly
Pressed by my fingers in their delivery

Got to get down these moments of clarity
These pieces of me
Each with a feeling and a memory

Needling nerve endings like a ringing phone
Each alone, but together a symphony.

8/3/06

This Child of Nine-Eleven

Born with the breaking of metal and glass,
I passed through an orifice like a TV screen
Into the bright sheen of a media campaign
Red white and blue red white and blue
As I tumbled to the checkerboard floor in the hospital
Where spin doctors picked me up and cooed
"The truth. The truth. The truth," they said,
"Is that we love you, our sweet consumer"

Rumor has it my garden is full of terror plots
Tilled by fingers that linger over vulnerable power plants
And spots where scant defense lines are scratched in dry soil.
Hot days are spent rubbing oil beneath straw hats
Buzzed by military flybys
Spies are everywhere
Terror is everywhere
Blooming like white convolvulus, weaving its way into desert sands
Abrams are jammed in a bad gag commute
Hands, tied by ticker tape news,
Outline the rise (and fall) of the price of crude,
Imply democracy while others pay our rent.
Let's portray sporadic resistance
(Turn your head and cough)
Then in the distance the bombs go off
And everyone bows down to our (fallen) monument

(Cue theme music)

Five years on with my umbilical still attached
I come back to TV for warmth,
Your glow of digital manipulation.
Mama mama mama
Don't abandon this child
Stay with me stay with me stay with me
Keep me awake, keep me abreast
With news breaks and shakes of paranoia
Amid earthquakes and floods and the falling stars

Keep me safe in my shell
Keep me safe in my shell
Keep me safe in my shell.

9/12/06

Out Here

Walking on the footpath
Under the fir trees
Between the sparse grass
Past the fat cat yacking a hairball
Watching the Latina hoop earrings and cleaning baskets
The white roofs and wet garbage cans
The patient impatient cars cars cars
Flat faces swollen and staring
Behind the spans of frosted curtains.

12/12/06

Hobo Sam

Sam rode in the box car hay with the skin of livestock
From Kansas City to Orleans
Nursing the smell of dung from his wool coat
Half asleep rocked by the train
Half awake jolted by gaps between wrought tracks

Hunger kept him company
His death face appearing
Stubble filling the sunken spaces

Children and spouses were left like stations several stops back
In days that appeared through cracks in the sliding doors
And nights that swallowed him whole

He used to hum to pass the time
But he only remembered one chorus of one tune
And the sound of "Oh Suzannah" made him remember the miles
So he stopped and practiced smiling

Sam rode in the hay from Orleans to Kansas City
Hiding with the sheep
Hands in their dung
Half asleep smothered by wool
Half awake waiting for the doors to open in daylight.

2/21/07

headline hangover

flagging words flapped in political filibusters,
distilled into dawn distributed data drops
slap paper handshakes folded in stacks,
branded and banded on cold paper stands

guttural rubbish runs close to the curb
disturbed by the murmur of street walkers,
bike messengers swerve through their verbal cud
between herds of streetcars and buses grinding their baseline,
the stony streets rumble from their flow

music bakeries waft notes in the chill cacophony,
a shiver of art on a sliver of concrete
makes for contralto breakfast before the news breakdown
in the town of hard-ons and come downs,
phalluses of glass and steel protruding and teeming
pointing to a sky that stares vacantly blue.

2/26/07

<u>morning arrival</u>

we barely move in the aluminum tube
rebreathing the air of hundreds before
and when the doors slide open
we overflow the tile platform
rushing escalators and stairs
a reverse waterfall.

2/27/07

rapture redux

telltale toner photocopies the free world
as legalities and clauses shop at ross
mismatched socks walk the checkerboard corridor
under holy cows and sacred drips

the tea sips under shawls before the wrestling knockdown
top hats tip for the shuffle of expository clowns
channel surfing wipe outs burst the beer keg bubble
college students scrutinize caramel covered cleavage lumps

hotel hellhole in a baghdad camel hump shootout
silent speaker phones stare blown out by psychoactive brawls
brass band shindigs gang banging the tuba tube sock baseline
base camp assaults on a contraband blasting cap

derelict dumpster hauls lost in the kabala junk heap
celebrity death wishes caught in crossfire suicide pacts
actors benign motions masturbate corporate riff-raff financiers
spliff smoke chokes the eyesore split screen slow-mo replay

half a day is enough to scuff the shoe black newness from your chaps

maitre d' handshakes the clambake smoke of the guest check replay
levitating stingrays strike the heartthrob lynch mob in its hour of need
censored greed chokes words right out of my cerebellum
leaving lily pad liftoffs bleeding bravely in frog pond graves.

Cut to commercial

Scene 1 ext day - outside jelly mold's candy home

Theme Song:
happy happy happy hoppy
hoppy hoppy hoppy hoop
sappy sappy sappy soppy
soppy soppy soppy soup
pappy pappy pappy poppy
poppy poppy poppy poop

                                                            Fade in:

Bunny suited underpaid actor jumps perkily toward the candy cane gate, wicker basket full of multicolor pastel eggs and flicks the sugar door latch and scratches his rabbit crotch. Crocheted curtains part to show the pseudo-plucky girl in red pigtails stare outside and roll her eyes.

POV hothouse rabbit suit:

The lolly swirl door opens and girl with blue checkerboard dress and white pinafore bounces in view with double-barreled shotgun knockers and circle blush on pale cheeks.

                                                                                                        Cut to:

                      RONNIE RABBIT
Hi! I'm Ronny the Rabbit. You must be Sue!

                              SUE
(chewing gum and twirling it on her thumb)
                            Uh huh.

                      RONNIE RABBIT
             Have you been a good girl?
I have happy eggs for all the good boys and girls!

                              SUE
                            Uh huh.

                    RONNIE RABBIT
             Here. Have a pretty pink one!

Ronnie hands over a large pink egg in his costume mitts to Sue's French manicured paws. A bit of gum string sticks to his fur.

                              SUE
                       (non plussed)
                           Thanks.

                    RONNIE RABBIT
           (Shaking free of the gum string)
Okay Sue! Have a happy super double-plus good Easter!

Sue rolls her eyes and closes the door

                                                                               Cut to:

Ronnie Rabbit in his worn brown costume hops out the candy gate up the windy road. He stops and scratches his crotch and turns to wave at Sue in the jelly mold house.

                           Cut to:

Sue in the window stares back and gives him the bird as she masticates with her mouth open.

                           Cut to:

Ronnie the rabbit shrugs his shoulders and hops out of frame with the candy cane house in the idyllic background. Suddenly the house explodes.

Ominous theme music

                       Fade to black

           ANNOUNCER VO
   Kids, never take candy from strangers.
Brought to you by the Department of Homeland Security
And now back to our regularly scheduled program...

             3
             2
             1

the sacred and holy shindig shivers with rapture spasms before the revival revealing recent conversions to fascist eating ho-ho ho-hums, white comatose pawns come kneeling on the pews perfectly passing time before the gaggle of god's castoff robe wearers review the guest list gore fest before the brimstone buffet, sashay in the finale theme song segue way to the polywoggle breakdown simulcasting simian hand jobs that boggle the syphilitic zoo station

nations have waited for the rim of the sun to trim their firebird mantra only to be left briquettes from the sons of their plethora

Brought to you by Kingsford charcoal: Lights first. Lights fast.

Stay tuned for Paris Hilton in "Bottoms Up".

3/1/07

<u>the pileup</u>

a cow moos a tune
imitating a horn
in the bovine traffic jam
on the grass overpass
noses rammed
bumper to bumper
at the toll gate
methane fumes collecting
in the daily payment
milked from their blood work.

3/2/07

this birthday

this birthday i will run barefoot in the park
dodging goose droppings and soggy crumbs
the bums use for croutons on grass salads

this birthday i will lie naked in my hammock
while macramé strings belgian-waffles my backside
and the southerly wind points my nipples skyward

this birthday i will walk on the beach, pant cuffs rolled
sidestepping the jellyfish, the kelp,
the old tui bottles left by bonfire revelers

this birthday i will ride a horse through the domain
scaring the students in their morning routines
as i grip the reins for dear life

this birthday i will run through the rain and the sun and the wind and the
clouds and the rain in the minutes between morning tea and lunch

this birthday i will take claratyne so i can smell the roses
bunched in my garden between the hording horny bees

this birthday i will eat cake and ice cream and ice cream and cake

this birthday i will hold life, give it a shake
then rake the fallen leaves tomorrow.

3/2/07 (for RA)

Nebraska (The Fall Back)

The stainless turbo prop striped in red, white and blue
Shook in a southwesterly blown across the salted tarmac.
Propellers spun in a Utah sputter, shuddering California
Until the plane rolled over the oil stains away from the tall window

The blue skies were grey in Nebraska
Overcast snapshots taken in wide angles
Rough stubble of clear cut corn fields
Drowned in sauces and mayonnaise
Steaks marinated for 24 hours in a whiskey still
The silt was slow to wash away

With Nebraska came the fall back.
Instead of spring there was snow,
No sun, only the bright fridge light,
Rustic décor and bear shaped handles,
Forrest wallpaper darkened by blackout curtains

At night I swam against the tide in the tepid pool
And reached the far rock edge
Where I toweled off and walked barefoot
Treading silently in the back hallways
Dripping my respite like evidence along the carpeted path.

4/16/07

Awake in Dallas in the Light Hotel

Awake in Dallas in the Light Hotel
The weight of bed sheets holds me down
This envelope sends me towards unconscious outlines
Where new insights clash with old advice
And past pages burn by firelight

Awake in Dallas in the Light Hotel
Motives are moved into long-term storage
And huddle on the corner of the street
Sharing their heat with bits of glass
Passed by cracks in the concrete path

Awake in Dallas in the Light Hotel
A welterweight starved to bone thickness
With sick breaths extends black hands
Wrapped with duct tape and plastic bags
Asking for one more chance to fight

Awake in Dallas in the Light Hotel
The wood and plaster secrete their smell
Tiles still shed their stone dust
Washing in repetition only makes them dull

Awake in Dallas in the Light Hotel
Heads are covered in shame
As games are played to pass the time

Awake in Dallas in the Light Hotel
The clock stares with red eyes

Awake in Dallas
In the Light Hotel
I wait for darkness.

4/26/07

not here (upstairs)

i don't find my mother here
where slick movements mesh
behind overdone underwear
sliding bra straps over nipples
nuptial motions sucking lobes
holes opening as old as productive urges
twisted pant legs chucked on the wool weave floor
drapes parted halfway
the shades cutting our bodies into slices
us fighting the limits of skin and skein
coiled like snakes under the striped duvet
arms that pull and hips that push
forgotten hinges and gaps
synapses snapping up motoneuron spaces
between coming home and the school bus horn
in the quick flesh hot breaths
of the locked suburban upstairs

released from our dog chain restraint
we lose memory for a moment
and regain the young days before distance and drudgery
our forgotten faces pressed down like reflections
once again open to be drowned.

12/27/07

<u>wandering beats</u>

although i'm partial to the use of rhyme,
and from time to time i like to wander, i think timing is key,
the tick tock stick of words in my teeth,
smacking red gums chewing asynchronous chomps chipped from stone leaves
wound around the pointed head of the painted fountain,
snapping rhythms of water slapping the backs of frozen green fish
who thrash the still life scene until peacocks preen their fans
and plead beside borderline bougainvillea hedges
locked in rusted wrought iron gates

missteps and breaks are made walking alone
along split asphalt paths under top-heavy century trees
lean willow leaves stroke the constant clear skin of the low avon
running in slow motion past the black teeth of the rough stone banks.
ducks and fish swim and splash on the ribbon of shallow green
rippling the water near the gondolas floating lazily by
the sky a glowing gray behind the branches of kowhai and cordyline
interspersed with fir and pine shelter canopies

couples garnish the rectangular grass, kids pass balls in open fields,
cricket matches and rugby games are played to measure time
as rhythm and rhyme footstep past in their own scene
leaning into each stride caught tapping
leaving the mind to dream of days in the garden
clapping to the beat of idyllic happiness.

2/7/08

Night is a Casual Friend

Night is a casual friend.
Come and go, night,
Stay for a while.
Here, have a drink.
Smile and tell me the lies of the city
In the fluent background rumble of the living:

In the seething love of the body
   shaped like San Miguel hills in neon curves
In the Polk Gulch alleys of piss and dumpsters
   slipped between ever-lit storefronts
In the stainless First street lobbies and gated condos
   packed with rich, young automatons
In the bunches of leather pressed clothes
   passing through the doors of dark SoMa bars
In the headlight choke of cars and buses
   sparking a thousand horizontal facets
In the steam and smells of fried meat
   blown into rising clouds over hilly Chinatown
In the statues and sand gripped by crabgrass
   slept on by bums in the worn corner park
In the random clatter of streetcars
   heralded by bells and stone shuddering

In the pointed intersections of diagonal avenues
In the phallic towers clustered downtown
In the din of 24 hour Haight Street record stores
In the smoke of hookah bars and Middle-Eastern trance
In the dance and clink of Italian coffee shops
In the sidewalk cafes lit by the glow of cigarettes
In the tenderloin on the crowded steps of mercy churches
In the fish decay and seagulls huddling on the wharf
In the crush of stuccoed duplexes and Victorian homes
In the stacked solo apartments of lone microwave meals

Lies appeal to you,
And you shelter them.
Night, don't be still,
Come and go.
You are my casual friend.

2/12/08

the drift

plastic keys try to please me
at my metal desk by boxes of energy
the lcd placates in crisp pixelation
electromagnetic paranoia signals in waves
printers exhale toner and ozone
the phone blinks red codes saying,
"you know where you are with"
ham-fisted emotions punching holes
reasons and opinions stolen from the road

at the metal wayside you wet your sleeve
then you left (or did i leave?)
hammering discontent repeatedly
in flexing muscles, twitching signs
smithing warm iron into edges, sparks
preparing to point the tip at me,
shield in place, marked with crosses
a mace hanging off your hip

my totality is left in young feet
some walking upside down under a summer lamp
faces blurred by watery heat
my voice just an echo
vibrating in their memories

some days i try to grow wings
to look down on roads like brittle veins
where metal blood pumps and pushes
gray with smoke from the crucible heart
cold clouds part as i drift past
i visit plots where old houses stood
their smashed walls now dust
to be swept up in clumps under the rug
afternoons spent trusting
questions thrust in naked revelation
become cold slides used only for dissection

in the evenings on the oversized sectional
separated by digital noise
digital remorse

we drift downstream
lights dimmed
children deaf in their sleep
you snoring under faux fur
me holding the remote
purple cushions sliding loose
sliding slowly to the floor
while i fold vertical distance with my eyelids.

2/28/08

<u>exit</u>

pack and get dressed before all hell breaks loose
before clocks are thrown at walls or stolen
before your B movie roles
make coasters for repeated cups of black
your bladder trembling in reruns
where children play in backgrounds backwards
hoping you choke on your joke

show me awake as i want to see it
bright blurs in the first seconds of day
adjoining beds parked in parallel
pass forever in space, stars wash into gray
watercolors and soapstone
don't lose your nerve
i can't do this alone

motorways move us in clover leaf outlines
blessing the foot that crushed your shell
burned gaps in chemical reactions
pain cracked pressure points
and bloomed like a firebird
swallowing everything in one bite
doors pried open by the jaws of life

bridge to the middle of afterwards
treasure island, yerba buena
missions and handfuls of orange clay
coastal highways blurred by fog
escape is just through the valley
through poppies and cristatum folds
the slopes sucked dry after the cold

hills stumble to the foot of the plain
as raindrops chatter with tempered glass
lightning dictates still life flashes
stored by wind witch and saguaro
snatches of lost time beaten by blows
my neck cramps looking over my shoulder
your rear view recedes as fast as we go

i watched the back of promises
heads rolled in long hauls of shame
desert hordes of torn clouds leaking darkness
windowless homes with open porches
corrugated roofs, corroded holes
i've driven on black ribbons tied like robes
banded tighter, cleaving hills,
clasping gas stations like glossy jewels

this is my final alarm, my last close
dreams tangled with lost sheets
scratch woolen blankets
open windows only blow cold
snow dusts still streets and roofs
the landscape sheds skin flakes
clustered on the edge of cracks
iron dirt frozen in the wind chill

this map unfolded traces veins
back to the heart, bordered by skid marks
boxes hold only enough to be carried
loads of paper words crumpled and folded
our sum totals divided once more
fescue grass points through white flecks
green fingers showing us where we go
as they hold broken bottles.

3/5/08

trance siberian

days were missed alone on the train
slipped between planks in platzkart bunk beds
passed by nodding heads intoxicated
with just enough samovar tea to wet cracked lips

coal smoke combed through clothes and hair
mixed with rolled fags chewed in silver teeth
vodka-stained canvas sacks gorging junk
lugged by traders in tri-color track suits

table crumbs, sardines and beer spills under elbows
cans of salat, condensed milk, eekra,
grease-stained newsprint piroshkees
all bought through the window at the last reprieve

you willed her face there under the pillow
to occupy you through broken sleep
through the rocking clatter of tracks
blue-sweatered conductor checks
grey skinned drunks
prodding away your novelty
davai americanyetz
drink drink
eesho eesho

but at the end you stepped off into snow
into the spring-loaded taxi ride
that propelled you to your dorm room
to the strip mined soleness
(sometimes called edeenstvo)
in the concrete blocks of a siberian afterglow.

3/19/08

this thaw

as in the past, the prod pushes us
shaven sheep assemble in the pen
promised sunlight
the full thaw
mutton breath stretches stiff legs
stunted grass
men and their dog teeth
bark before the inevitable slaughter

the farmhouse leans forward
wooden ribs exposed
to watch the wet stare of spring.

4/24/08

<u>there is music in hell</u>

there's music in hell
it is elevator music
because everything is going down
the place is a mess
cauldrons are cracking
boilers are on their last legs
even the forks are split
the devil is a corrupt dictator
minions argue and conspire
people are screaming
but there is music
with sax
and violins.

4/26/08

<u>there sex is</u>

trees there sex is
in the lusty buds
opening petals
pollen brings bees is

intercourse mixed is
swollen fermentation
eggs warmed in the nest
juices secreted is

the chemicals coursing is
blood working the flesh
stimulate under fingertips
the curve into hips is

undulated valleys and hills
folded in sheets is
rolled and twisted is
exhalations of sated lips.

4/28/08

stone mountain

granite slopes like a dome
like a serving of mashed potatoes
when i walk off comfort food
up the uneven water-worn path.
used fat evaporates
each step made under stubborn pines
each once just the idea of a tree
standing still in a stone crack
when sherman burned this town

i rise on the back of confederacy
where snow hardly falls
and bob, tom, and jeff watch tourists
interbreed and shoot off lasers,
their rock hard resolve
broken not by the elements
but by the blood of kin folk
freshened with bayonets
and crushed by memory into bright iron soil

i wipe oil from my forehead
as a way to exhale
as a way to climb above these plains
so stated in phrases of sharp gasps
rising always rising
to the gondola's final stop
where school kids and breathless riders
eat hot dogs and take photos
framed by the frayed southern skyline.

5/16/08

Rubber Soles

When I walk
All I see are shoes
Two days of moving through town
And shoes look at me
Like kids stare at dinosaur bones
Backpack stuffed and worn
Shuffling to the coffee shop
Pockets clinking with change
My jacket seams all but given up

At least summer's coming
When evenings stay like blankets
Soft beds of grass
Beer bottles almost half-full
County fairs and sidewalk stores
Summer shoes stare at me
Sometimes pointing open toed
Tongues panting in the heat
Painted lids, pedicures
Pretty flowered sandals

At least summer's coming.
I'll bathe in the river
Just at sunrise
Before light makes me transparent
I'll wash my clothes, dress the branches
And dry myself on the riverbank
Until I shrink and become vapor
Rising from the earth to fall
Slowly in a shower or with fury in a storm
Only still to be trampled by countless rubber soles.

5/27/08

Post Mortem

All the way, the phone call shook
Dividing goodbyes into discrete sounds
Slicing all the grounds of coffee evenings
Caffeine reverting to molecules
Mixed with plasma,
Dopamine, norepinephrine
The brain inhaled my cocktail and coughed
Words spilled out in reply
One mass of apologies

It's easy to say there is still time
To try new equations, new concoctions
Mixtures of old and new melodies
Songs to wear like jackets or shoes
It's easy to think there is still time
To lose inhibitions in the living room
To find attraction over the smallest things
To bring sentiment back into hands, eyelids
Walks up the hill at night

It's easy to dissect moments
Into individual tissues and flesh
Tendons and nerves
Scalpel steady hand on the lab bench
It's easy to dissect sentences
Nouns, pronouns, verbs
Mechanical parts and design
A classroom whiteboard diagram
The skeleton of language

It is easy for silence to outline spaces
It is easy for silence to fill up spaces
It is easy for silence to smother details
When all is said and done
When the corpse is cold
You can cut across it and count the rings
Notations and analysis
Scribbles of your pen
Glancing over dark rims

The call ends before the shock
Humectants in my ocular sockets
Formaldehyde occultists hold me
This stainless bed
Cold sheets
My blood removed.

6/4/08

the shoreline

you walked without shoes up the shore
navigating gull droppings,
ground glass, jellyfish,
missed the washed up castles
and a pink shovel left like a sundial

you walked a nautical mile
feet dug into sand just above the waterline
fine time squeezed between metacarpals
the earth conducting energies
directly into your pectoralis majoris

ocean spectrums of sound
sprayed auditory static in the airwaves
flotsam frothed lapping at crab graves
water tongues wagged in passing,
atomized salt crystals stung your skin

the sideways sun skint on heat
still made you squint as you looked back
sands stretching into infinite shoreline
your grass hat brim folded
halos crossed on your retinae

from my lookout your form wavered
white flag scarf waving
the sky mist wandered inland
my towel island sliding ever closer to the sea
as i watched you flicker me goodbye.

6/24/08

Spells

Synapses fire in spray patterns
Suggesting stretched siestas on the sofa
Sunday afternoons caressed with fan breezes
Parasympathetic impulses, dust motes
Passed into hands stroking
The sacrum, fused and soft

Your light skin hair stands against my fingertips.

7/6/08

the crane pose

planets are aligned today.
gravity balances force
directly in proportion
and inversely proportional
to distances between them
measured in arm lengths.
dynamic equilibrium
seizes the order of things

commitments, counter-commitments,
millstones, gallstones, the moon,
holding patterns pulling limbs,
pinpricks and cold space
place equations
imaginary numbers
opposite me in the hallway mirror
like divisions into infinitesimals

i observe the order of things
desires equalized into stasis
stillness, two opposite pulls,
magnetic poles of earth
stabilized by lunar-spin:
tidal motions, hemispherical seasons,
reasons to close the windows
or mow the lawn shirtless

and once order is found and held
couches pose at angles
facing digital reasoning,
directives to consume or imbibe
wavered by whim and suggestion,
balance sways flexing muscles,
sinews stretch and pull aside
waiting for worlds to collide.

8/6/08

<u>your new proportion will keep her happy</u>

low self esteem from a small weenie,
wiener, little vienna sausage?
erase all the memories of your greatest defeats
graduate in style with a new shaft
and impress her with your manly manhood

put a huge sausage in her bun
have fun all night long with your big shlong
celebrate a victory in love
your performance and mastery will satisfy
transform into a sex god
start today and you'll be on top.. and behind ...and in front

bewitch her with your thick love snake
make her ride your rigid rod
a rocket dong pleases girls
mega-size your johnson today
why wait? rake in the girlfriends

you don't have to be resigned to your short pete
get longer, harder and more robust pole meat
women crave a larger tool so they can feel satisfied
be bigger, be greater than ever before
cram your man spam in to her clam
and make her come to you forever.

8/8/08

the face on the stairs

there is a face that sits on the stairs
balanced on the oak banister
it looks at me and watches the tv i watch
it waits for me to see

i close the blinds to keep out the heat
even though summer is ending
even though the foliage is thick and the branches have grown
i close the blinds to keep out the heat

hours dwindle into minutes seconds
the days into hours
the months into days
and again again time is a sink of water emptying

taken twice daily, swallowed
suffering can give life meaning
just like glass lightly heated, eaten twice
only some sand burnt into clarity

a hate lives close to this jar
close to the bus rides with mother
close to the car rides with the ex
close to my hands clenched

smells of burning signal the end
smoldering self sorrow
puffs of hot air, smoke rings signal
stay away stay away stay away
there is a reason to turn the lights off
night lies like a dark line
wormed in iron red soil
rolled in perpetual prayer crying,
"i want to die
i want to live
i want to emerge
i want to disappear"

there is a face that watches me from the stairs
it waits for me to go up.

8/13/08

<u>the common communion</u>

bells do not ring here
as time genuflects sweating skin
swearing simian genes symbolize
invitational thighs flexing
the riot of civilization

a nipple twist sparks chemicality
lists of causation down potassium gates
blood makes heat, the blush flows
friction sweat wetting nerve wires
electrical dendrite trees shiver delight

there are horny toads thrusting legs
pinned by eyes in ether bliss
hearts pulse to latino rhythms
the misms of mystical brain stem seduction
pant legs drop mesmerizing memory

immaculate breaths caress necklines
cracks to suggest progenation
succulent curvatures bend the horizon
mountains valleys lactate rivers
testosterone flash flood angry divinities

make me please, knees bending
dark nods to the god of oblation
velvet pews, lips pursed
makeshift slow immolation, redemption
victimized impaling climax catechism

armor calcinates into holy weakness
invitations to enter, penetrate
entrails digesting enzymes
divine failures, soft holds
as unearthed we negotiate.

8/19/08

<u>holy rolled</u>

the praise the praise the praise
faces full of God-bound hyperbole
displaced from rice thin pages
padded tube steel seating
painted wall panels reverberate
music, spun cloth, ejaculations,
tongues motivated by electricity

the J man gospel megaphone waver
preaches in all the kingly ways
the songs the verses the melody
flush ambivalence from full ears
round orifices resonate with echoes
multiplied amplified verities
focused to animate the dull and grave

glory gold, whole word holy
verbal blessings, aggressive grace
addressing dynamic congregation holds
pressing hands into joins, clapping palms
plates transform into tambourines
and silence is waived by dancing legs and arms
where once the charms of a quiet God were praised.

8/25/08

Hightower's last meal

four fried pork chops
collard greens with boiled okra
fried corn
fried fatback
fried green tomatoes
cornbread
lemonade
one pint of strawberry ice cream
three glazed donuts

it starts with snorted coke which gives me the edge
the snub nose i already loaded and slipped in our bed
then two whiskeys, the cheapest i could get,
four beers, a wine, and a tequila chaser
my guilt is already drunk when i leave the bar

the bitch and her little bitches exchange looks
but keep quiet like they do after dinner
Sandy watches Cosby and Eve has her Harlequin
i hold the paper up and reread the comics
while Dot washes dishes and then puts the squeaker to bed

i'm gonna end it for them
it'll be tonight, the bitching will be done.
then i'll drive east through Augusta
and maybe see the coast
maybe put my feet in the sea at Kiawah Island

i'm gonna end it tonight
their lights are going out
and i'll spend summer evenings
swimming like i did when i was 12
diving into the arms of dark ocean waves
until the last of the sunlight dies.

8/26/08

<u>demotibilized</u>

olive green linoleum squares
laid in miles like government blankets
tiles of fluorescent days
seamless pine sol footsteps
clock arms signal slow-motion warnings
monotone communication
servants as civil as metronomes
measured paper molehills
grown in folders into stone edifices
licensing leashes and tags
sand bags and hedgerows
slowly rolled on this conveyor belt
silt feet and sweat mix
affixed to number B1056.

10/13/08

An American Stain

This noose is hanging from a lamppost
An open mouth in the sweaty green tree rows
White shirt sleeves perspiring
Midnight smiles divided in columns
Doric, Ionic lines, brick facades
Willows drag branches at the riverbank
Birch and Aspen strangled by faceless ivy
Rusted dirt like a scab in the undergrowth

Who knows what seed has grown
Sown behind picket fences
Beer bottles, brown telescopes
Sport teams wrapped in red and black
Fried cookouts and firearms
Trapped and covered in graphs and gaffing tape
Country crooners twang and refrain
Hiding the depth of this American stain.

10/13/08

<u>time warp</u>

brick monochrome make-outs
70s thighs, drumstick beats
fumbles in the back of Vauxhalls
fine times rolling fags, smoking crowns
stolen highs in the upper downs
highballs, pints, cheap wine
time to spend collared years waiting
to evolve beyond wife-beaters and clotheslines
pretzel sticks and savouries
smeared with sleepless nights
worn corridors blighted
smouldering days to their butt ends
red eyes hotwired
seaside salts and croaking gulls
sand and endless cold sea
horizons like dotted lines
perforated
torn by love
and spray
and the memory of clear sky.

1/22/09

<u>hungry</u>

dry fried chicken devoured in foil
incisors tear, molars grind
sounds of crunching smacking
a ritual by hours salivating
oily fingers, old thirsts

our first kiss, the hallway watched,
your mom's berkeley bungalow
sniffed old joints and plaster
hollow signs of parenthood
on the three light projection tv

you punched i kicked
sibling struggles before breakfast
mothers, whores, sisters
all spectators
hoarse cheering

hardened edges of fingers, feet
now cut to the chase
chopping motions walk
the corner liquor store
destined to be numb

i chew
i swallow.

1/27/09

I have a nothing box

You cleared out your things
Anonymous cardboard
Permanent reminders
Labeled black letters
Your last will
Washed dishes stacked in the rack
Drying shiny flowers

Dust motes float by the lamp
Sub-freezing frost clouds outside
My arrival blows condensation
Carpets rolled aside
Tied with twine
Tidy dry tongues

Daylight stumbles
As dark hues stick and slide
Bare walls, hardwood footsteps.
You sweep the last of your memory
Kitchen cleaning
Pine oil, plastic buckets

Silence is a cracked vase
Placed in the bin
With book covers
Perfume bottles
Down feathers
Holed socks
Q-tips
Crumbs
Dust

The rusted gate speaks one last time
And freezes shut
A perfect cut-out
Preserved in the heart of our empty album.

2/5/09

<u>drive by</u>

bang
the poem is shot
magazine ink spots
dykes with spoons
ragtime ice cream
carbon dust
pickup sticks
barnacles
twist ties
hairpins
pencils
lists
endless lists.

1/20/09

<u>the end of poetry</u>

my head is a plastic bucket
stuck in space on a spinning rock
it wobbles heavy in a downpour
and in dry times it gapes
a patient exclamation
"O".

1/6/09